For Anne
Best Wishes

John Rogge

The
Tao
of
Spirit

BOOKS BY JOHN-ROGER

Awakening Into Light
Baraka
Blessings of Light
The Christ Within & Disciples of Christ
with the Cosmic Christ Calendar
The Consciousness of Soul
A Consciousness of Wealth
Dream Voyages
Drugs
Dynamics of the Lower Self
Forgiveness—Key to the Kingdom
God Is Your Partner
Inner Worlds of Meditation
The Journey of a Soul
Loving...Each Day
Manual on Using the Light
The Master Chohans of the Color Rays
Passage Into Spirit
The Path to Mastership
Possessions, Projections & Entities
The Power Within You
Q&A from the Heart
Relationships—The Art of Making Life Work
Sex, Spirit & You
The Signs of the Times
The Sound Current
The Spiritual Family
The Spiritual Promise
Walking with the Lord
The Way Out Book
Wealth & Higher Consciousness

CO-WRITTEN WITH PETER MCWILLIAMS
DO IT!
LIFE 101
You Can't Afford the Luxury of a Negative Thought
WEALTH 101
We Give to Love

FOR FURTHER INFORMATION, PLEASE CONTACT:
MSIA®
P.O. Box 3935, Los Angeles, CA 90051
(213) 737-4055

The
Tao
of
Spirit

JOHN-ROGER

Published by Mandeville Press
P.O. Box 3935
Los Angeles, CA 90051

Printed in the United States of America

I.S.B.N. 0-914829-33-5

FOREWORD

This book was inspired by the *Tao Te Ching*, a book written by Lao-Tzu in the sixth century B.C., and is a collection of writings by John-Roger that are designed to help you let go of this world and return to the stillness within.

The *Tao of Spirit* is arranged in eighty-one chapters, as is the *Tao Te Ching*, but it stands alone, and knowledge of the *Tao Te Ching* is not necessary as you read this book. Nevertheless, students of the Chinese classic may find that John-Roger's writing enhances their understanding of it.

The chapters of the book can be read as daily or weekly inspiration. They can be read in order or selected randomly. They are a wonderful way to start the day or to end the day by reminding you to let the world go. In its simple way, the book can provide a new way of approaching day-to-day problems and frustrations, and it also can be used as preparation for meditation, contemplation, prayer, or spiritual exercises. Because it encompasses so much, to me, it is a book to live by.

Lao-Tzu was a Mystical Traveler, one who has a direct line of energy into the Divine and is aware of that connection and maintains it. As John-Roger has said, "The reality as brought forward by the Traveler Consciousness is that everything is perfectly present right now."

A few years ago, when I was putting together a workshop called the "Tao of the Travelers" for Peace Theological Seminary and College of Philosophy, I had a meeting with John-Roger to discuss it. In the meeting, I asked him whether he could tell me anything about Lao-Tzu. (I knew from my studies that virtually nothing reliable existed about Lao-Tzu's life, so here, I thought, was an opportunity to finally know something about the man.) Unfortunately, it was not a day where Lao-Tzu was about to reveal too much about himself. However, J-R did relate the following:

> What I would say about Lao-Tzu could be said about all the Travelers: They are people for their times, though they are not really in the times. So for Lao-Tzu to contact the people he was sent to reach, he would have to come to them in such a way that they would be able to recognize him as somebody they themselves could reach back to. So, if it was necessary, he would have to whore with the whores and drink with the drunks. Now, if Lao-Tzu had

to reach a butcher—if that person was one of his to get, out of this lifetime—he would have to go and work alongside him, so that the butcher would awake and say, "Who are you, really?" Then Lao-Tzu would reveal himself and would start to teach that person by the method of the times.

The Travelers come forward to point the way to our true home, which is in Spirit. Yet, as John-Roger has said many times, "As soon as I open my mouth or write it down, I have 'lied' to you because the spiritual truths cannot be spoken." In this book, you will find many paradoxes and contradictions. The essence is found in the space between the words. You may ask, "Then why have a book?" Perhaps the answer is that if the words weren't there, how could we find the spaces?

Paul Kaye
September 1994

And I say to any man or woman, Let your soul stand cool and composed before a million universes.

Walt Whitman

One

There is no path in spiritual progression.
There just is spiritual progression.
When people talk about 'a path,'
they set up distance
and a sense of beginning and ending.
That's a fallacy.
There's no beginning,
no ending,
and no separation.

We are all spiritual by our very natures.
One person is not more spiritual than another,
regardless of behavior, intelligence, ability,
   or anything else.
All those things may affect the expressions in a
   person's life.
They do not affect the person's spirituality.

Two

*I*f we, indeed, pay attention,
even for one day out of our lifetime,
and we are, indeed, thoughtful and intuitive,
and we are watching very carefully
where we're putting our mind
and our emotions
and our body,
we might not get much done that day in the
    physical, emotional, mental world,
but we would deliver ourselves
from eons of karma.

Three

He who binds to himself a joy
Does the winged life destroy;
But he who kisses the joy as it flies
Lives in eternity's sunrise.

William Blake

"Let go and let God" is not a cliché.
It is a practical direction.
Is there any hurry to go anywhere?
Where are you going that you are not already there?
How can you be impatient
when the important things are always present?

If you want the spiritual flow to work unconditionally,
then you must let it flow unconditionally.
No modifications.
No conditions.
No deals.
Just keep it open.
You receive as openly as you give.
If you start qualifying,
you'll lose.

If you move from a state of tension,
you will be blocked.

If you always move
from your center of relaxation,
you will be free.

<u>Four</u>

*L*et each loving relationship you have with another
   human being
live primarily inside you.

If you place it in the world,
you will experience difficulty.

There's no relationship out there.
There is only the reflection
of what you are doing inside yourself
and how you're dealing with relationships inside
   of you,
not out there.

Five

Without going outside, you may know the whole world.

Lao-Tzu

*Y*ou cannot look into the world
for the fulfillment of desire
and look to Spirit at the same time.

It's a mirror.
You find that if you lust,
lust finds you.
If you seek sensation,
sensation finds you.
If you seek love,
love comes to you.

And if you stand within your own natural, neutral
space,
you are able to choose the time, the place, and the
extent of your participation.

The more you walk within your own rhythm,
the more you walk in the realization of your own God
consciousness,
no one will be able to "assassinate" you in any way.
You will be beyond those levels.
They will not be able to reach you.

Six

When the Guest is being searched for,
    it is the intensity of the longing for the Guest that
    does all the work.
Look at me, and you will see a slave of that intensity.

Kabir

*I*t's quite obvious that the Spirit doesn't care if it's fair
   or not fair.

In fact, I have found that Spirit seems to be ruthless.
Not that it cuts or hits at you,
but it's ruthless in the intent that if you're not very
   much focused towards it,
it does not indicate to you that it's there.

And after we go through trials, tribulations, and
   trouble to get back inside,
and then it doesn't say hello or anything,
it can seem like a gross unfairness
compared to the amount of time and effort we have
   put into it.

Here's the paradox:
Spirit has always been here.
And for the most part,
it seems like we've always been here.

So if we've always been here
and it's always been here,
why are we not knowing
that we're both here?

What is this thing inside of us
that stops us from knowing
what's going on?

Seven

*Y*ou may not be turning to face Spirit enough to build up, hold, and expand your awareness to encompass the whole vista of the cosmos and its creation.

To be involved with that is an experience of now
because Spirit is always evolving,
devolving,
exploding,
and imploding
all at the same time.

It's chaos.
Out of the chaos comes creation in its finest state and
beingness.

But almost in the moment of its happening,
it's past.
It is an ongoing process.
Creation is always new in every moment.
What you focus and act upon is your creation.
As soon as you talk or think about it,
it's past.

Be willing to not know what's going on
so you can know what's going on.
Be willing to not know who you are
so you can find out.

<u>Eight</u>

*W*hy do you need recognition?

You say that you feel you need it.
Sacrifice your feelings.
You say that you think you need it.
Sacrifice your mind.
You say that you really do need it.
That's ego.
Sacrifice your ego.
What's left?
Nothing.
That nothing is exactly what you are, here on the
   planet.

All the partial games you play
attempt to make you something you're not.
What you are is no-thing,
and no-thing is the very essence of God present.

Nine

Though inland far we be,
Our souls have sight of that immortal sea
Which brought us hither.

William Wordsworth

*S*pirit is not a process of the outer world,
although its qualities may be reflected here
in kindness,
loving,
and compassion.

Spirit itself lives in the inner consciousness.
Its voice rings in the stillness of your heart.
Its movement is in the perfect stillness within.
Its greatest expression is in the peace and loving
that reside at the core of your beingness.

When you are attuned to Spirit,
there is nothing in the outer world that matters.
Even your negative thoughts and emotions don't
   matter.
They have no power at all in the presence of Spirit.
The negativity of others does not matter.
There is love and forgiveness—
for everything and everyone.

The more you are loving,
the more you free yourself
to experience the Soul.

Ten

Shape clay into a vessel;
It is the space within that makes it useful.

Lao-Tzu

*I*t is within the no-thing that the Spirit lives.

The Spirit will not come into a space that is already
   filled.
If you are filled with anxiety, fear, depression, and
   disturbance,
there is no space for the Spirit.
And since the Spirit cannot violate your
   consciousness,
it must stay outside.

When you give up the negative emotions and
   expressions,
the space that is left can be filled by the Spirit.
But you must create the space.

You have to risk letting go of the things that do not
   work for you
in order to gain the things that will.

Eleven

*Y*ou seem to forget your ability to see clearly
  the rules of the game you're supposed to master.
Not the game you're supposed to win,
but the game you're supposed to master.

Even the way you lose
can show that you've mastered the game.

Don't play games with yourself;
don't rationalize your deceptions,
thinking that no one notices.

It doesn't matter whether anyone else notices.
The Spirit that is God inside of you
knows your truth
and knows your deceit.

Keep in mind that the rules of humankind do not
  work when it comes to spiritual awakening.
If you learn nothing else from me,
please learn that.

Twelve

We walk silent among disputes and assertions, but reject
   not the disputers nor any thing that is asserted,
We hear the bawling and din, we are reach'd at by divisions,
   jealousies, recriminations on every side,
They close peremptorily upon us to surround us, my
   comrade,
Yet we walk unheld, free, the whole earth over…

                         Walt Whitman

*H*ow can you have understanding without first
   having acceptance?

You must accept the people around you.
You must accept the people out in the world.
You must accept the people who are killing other
   people.

Must.

For in this acceptance, you can control their
   slaughtering.
In your understanding, you can show them the way.
In your cooperation, you can lift the world.
And by your enthusiasm, the Soul walks alive in the
   human form.
You have then fulfilled the spiritual consciousness
   present.

But it will be hardly recognized
because the man of understanding is misunderstood.
For you cannot understand what it is
to have understanding.

Thirteen

*T*here is nothing in existence other than right now.

When we go into memory,
we're no longer present in the Spirit.
We're in a contraction of the mind and the emotions,
and it actually has no value for us.

The teaching of the world is of contraction.
The teaching of the Traveler is of expansion.

Fourteen

*I*f you start defending your illusion,
  you have to fight a battle that you're going to lose
    even if you win
  because it will eventually turn out that you are wrong.

Even if you fight and win,
you lose.
When you don't have to fight,
you are winning.

Fifteen

I exist as I am, that is enough,
If no other in the world be aware I sit content,
And if each and all be aware I sit content.

One world is aware and by far the largest to me, and
    that is myself,
And whether I come to my own to-day or in ten thousand
    or ten million years,
I can cheerfully take it now, or with equal cheerfulness
    I can wait.

Walt Whitman

*W*hen you observe,
you just state what you saw take place.
You say, "I saw this and this and this."
Somebody asks, "Was it that?"
You say, "I didn't see that."
They ask, "Did they do this?"
You say, "I didn't see that."
There is no need to even say, "I don't know,"
because that moves it out of the state of observation.

The statement of observation is only what is,
not what you know or don't know about the situation.

The power that comes from that, internally, is
 tremendous.
It becomes so nice that you just want to stay in that
 place.
And that's not a state of "do nothing."
The statement of neutrality and observation is an
 active place;
it doesn't carry any negative weight or positive weight
 for outcome.

Sixteen

*W*hen you are lazy and procrastinate, you expend
   more energy in emotional addiction than you
   would if you just went and did the physical thing
   that has to be done.

When things are handled,
the emotions quiet down,
and the mind becomes calm.

When things are handled moment by moment,
   you find out that everything is fine,
   everything is smooth,
   everything is right where it should be.

At this point,
nothing is disturbing your body.
And when you think of right now,
you don't want to jump off into the future
because right now is really quite nice.
You live here and now in this moment.

When you are handling everything that comes your way,
there is no past or future,
and the present is the eternal now.

Then there's only one way to go,
and that's up in consciousness
because everything around you
is kept in a state of maintenance.

Seventeen

*I*t is not necessary to worry or pressure yourself.
It all works out perfectly,
contrary to anyone's thought processes
or how they feel about it.

The challenge is to make your mind hold a focus
    until you complete the action of your thought.
If you learn only that,
you will have overcome this earth.

Eighteen

You have slept for millions and millions of years.

Why not wake up this morning?

Kabir

*Y*ou don't have to understand something that is
  already within you;
you just have to awaken to your experience of it.
Then understanding appears.

The sleeper goes for abundance
by manifesting illusion out of greed and insecurity.
The one who is awakened
only has to take in the next breath.

Nineteen

To gain awareness of Soul,
you move to each moment of divine beingness.
You don't let your mind disturb you,
and you don't let your emotions push you around.

You just breathe in
and breathe out,
holding the focus as the present action completes
itself.

You don't complete it.
I don't complete it.
The action of Spirit completes itself in its own timing.

Twenty

Ne'er saw I, never felt, a calm so deep!
The river glideth at his own sweet will!

William Wordsworth

*P*erfect your beingness by going slowly through the
routine of your life
until you have it mastered.

Do the ordinary things that make up your life.
Learn to do those things to the point of mastery.
You'll find great satisfaction in them.

Conduct your life from a place of quiet, calm loving.
Get it perfected so that the routine of your life does
not distract you or disturb you
and so you can maintain a state of loving in
everything you do.

Then you can expand the scope of your activity,
moving your loving heart out to others in a natural,
ordinary way.
Then you are just present with people, loving them.

Living your life in an ordinary way can be the most
tremendous service to your fellow men.

Twenty-one

The mere process of entering into comparisons says
   that you lost.
Comparisons have nothing to do with spiritual
   progress.

Get this clear:
Nobody out there can love you
the way you want to be loved.
Only you can do that.

Twenty-two

And I have felt
A presence that disturbs me with the joy
Of elevated thoughts; a sense sublime
Of something far more deeply interfused,
Whose dwelling is the light of setting suns,
And the round ocean and the living air,
And the blue sky, and in the mind of man:
A motion and a spirit, that impels
All thinking things, all objects of thought,
And rolls through all things.

William Wordsworth

*D*o you accomplish a lot here?
Probably not.
Then what's the value here?
The value here is not to accomplish a lot,
because it's all been accomplished.

Your job is to become aware of the divine presence
   within you,
which you are,
and to use this level to spring into higher
   consciousness.

That's what this level is about.
It's the springboard,
not the place you stay in.

Your job is easy.
You can extract yourself from any situation that you
   want to,
if you're willing to pay the sacrifice
   of giving up your greeds
   and your pride,
   and your lusts,
   and your envy,
   and your ego,
and just live purely in the moment.

Twenty-three

*W*ipe away the concept of "there."
Discard the idea that anything has to be present
   physically
to be manifest here and now.
Open your consciousness to the unmanifest reality,
in which all things are immediately present
and forever new.

How do you find without seeking?
How do you desire God
and make it desireless?

A desire for God is desireless
because it is unmanifest reality.

You can only desire that which is manifest,
and that desire becomes a trap.
It always has been.

Within the self is the knower.
That knower manifests total awareness
so that there is no searching,
no seeking,
and no yearning after that which is manifest.

Twenty-four

On this level, you don't grab.
You can't possess,
and you can't hold on to anything.

If you try to possess, you lose.
You can't even possess your own body.
But if you love yourself,
if you love the Soul within,
you have access to all things.

We shut down God by moving into the world,
professing God's greatness out there.
And we've lost track that God is inside us
    in the greatness.

Twenty-five

*Because someone has made up the word
'wave,' do I have to distinguish it
from water?*

Kabir

You observe the action of life in much the same way
as you observe a stream of water flowing down a
mountainside.
You just sit there and watch it.
You don't try to grab the last bit of water that went by.

It's the same as watching the ocean.
You don't try and grab the last wave and cement it
so that you'll always have it.
You just watch the waves come in and go out,
come in
and go out.

There is no boredom in watching the ocean
because your ego is not involved in what the waves do
or don't do.
You are observing.

Twenty-six

*O*nce we embrace the reality that all things are Spirit
and that the body, the emotions, and the mind
are all Spirit manifesting differently,
each doing their own nature,
we do not go against the nature.

We allow the nature to flow,
without being hung up in it,
without overly identifying with it.

Don't let yourself get confused,
when you have depressions, anxieties and frustrations
that you're sitting anywhere less
than in the presence of the Lord.

Twenty-seven

Silence is the perfectest herald of joy.

William Shakespeare

*W*hen people stop to listen
and the mind becomes quiet,
they sometimes will go to sleep out of habit.

The better choice is to hold yourself alert and awake
and to just listen.

Listen for whatever comes forward out of the silence.
Listen past the inner conversations of your mind.

If things start to distract and disrupt you,
bring your focus back to the silence.
As many times as the silence is broken,
you can refocus on listening to the silence
one more time.

When you bring yourself into the silence,
you can then experience the knowing and the wisdom
that will start flowing.

Then people often want to comment mentally on the
    experience,
or they feel a need to write it down.
But that in itself becomes a distraction that can shut
    off the silence.

Twenty-eight

*T*he essence is the essence.

It is now—and has always been—eternally present.
So you are never born,
and you never die.
All you do is focus your attention to whatever level
   you care to.

That to which you are attentive,
that which you're visualizing,
that upon which you focus your energy to alleviate
   stress, tension, and fear
—that brings you freedom.
It breaks the karmic blocks,
and you rise to a new level.

Twenty-nine

This day before dawn I ascended a hill and looked at the
*   crowded heaven,*
And I said to my spirit, When we become the enfolders of
*   those orbs and the pleasure and knowledge of every*
*   thing in them, shall we be filled and satisfied then?*
And my spirit said No, we level that lift to pass and
*   continue beyond.*

Walt Whitman

If you have a spiritual experience and you want to
    keep having spiritual experiences,
you must turn from that which you just completed
and go on to the next thing.

It doesn't matter how wonderful or uplifting your
    experience was;
you turn from that
and go on to the next thing.
To do less is to deny your growth and awareness.

As soon as you measure your present experience with a
    past experience,
you have judged it,
and your judgments will be upon you.
You have then propelled yourself out of Spirit.

To get yourself back into the Spirit,
you move into the present moment
and love whatever is happening.

When you are not living in expectation,
you can't be caught in negativity.

Thirty

To know what is spiritual in a situation,
you have to get above it,
not run any of your own stuff on it,
and move to a place of observation.

If you would just enter into observation,
you would be able to perceive so much more clearly.

From that state of observation,
you realize that there's nothing there.
You have nothing to gain or lose one way or another,
and it doesn't matter whether you are involved or not.
You'll be able to see things really clearly,
just for what they are.

And if you don't see something clearly,
you shouldn't assume anything about it,
because as soon as you assume anything, guess what?
You've moved out of observation
and you have your own stuff mixed up in there.

Thirty-one

I'll tell you a secret about this world:
it meets you exactly where it finds you
and gives you what you present to it.

So, if you go out there looking for anger,
it will justify your anger.
If you go out there looking for love,
it will justify your love.
If you're looking for animosity and hatred,
it will give you animosity and hatred.
It will match exactly what you put out.
That's the key if you want health, wealth, and
  happiness.

You can't go out there with animosity, anger, and greed
and expect it to give you something else.
It won't do that.

The Spirit will give you that which is your intention,
and the amazing thing is
you can't put your intention out here in the world.
It's for you and your own inner universe to live in.
And if you're not creating a healthy universe,
it will eventually get out here
and you'll have your catastrophe and disaster.
What are those?
Whatever people declare them.

Thirty-two

I wandered lonely as a cloud
That floats on high o'er vales and hills,
When all at once I saw a crowd,
A host, of golden daffodils.

William Wordsworth

*H*ave you ever smelled perfume from a flower?
That's similar to how the Spirit moves.
That flower was really nearby in order for you
   to smell it.
And if you turned toward that essence of perfume
and started tracing it back,
you came to the source it was coming from.
But you must pursue it in order to get to the source.

If the perfume seems to float interminably through
   the air,
you have more of a job.
You have to be more alert,
more aware,
more watchful than before.

And it could be that you smelled it for so long,
you've lost track that it's present.
But someone new coming in will say,
"That sure smells like roses,"
to once again refresh your mind of what you know.

And that's what I'm here for:
to once again refresh your mind of what you know.
You already knew all this,
and you didn't deal with it,
and it's okay if you don't deal with it now.

But my job is to tell you,
and that's what I'm doing.

Thirty-three

*U*nderstanding is your strength.

Being strong is not your strength.
Being strong could mean resistance,
and resistance could lead to separation,
and separation is the fear of death.

Strength is the understanding of your reality.
It is truth
and neither needs defense
nor is concerned about an attack of others' opinions.

Thirty-four

*I*f you deny something,
   that doesn't put it out of existence.
In fact, the act of mentally denying something
   actually affirms it
because you put energy into it
instead of letting it go.

The best way to let something go is just to stop
   participating in its energy field
and to go in another direction.
The thing or issue then ceases to be a source of
   distracting energy in your life.

Thirty-five

The fool doth think himself wise, but the wise man knows himself to be a fool.

William Shakespeare

*I*t takes a high degree of intelligence
to cooperate with what is going on.

In your mind, however,
you will usually not allow it to be like that.
You'll say that it is not so.

It is your attitude towards things
that either blocks you
or frees you.

Thirty-six

All men will come to him who keeps to the one,
For there lie rest and happiness and peace.

Lao-Tzu

The true master
realizes the opportunity
of oneness with God
in every experience,
in every human being,
and in every event.

Thirty-seven

*I*t's understanding that lifts the consciousness.
It's not *saying* understanding;
it is *living* understanding,
it is *doing* understanding,
it is where, in the midst of misery,
you still have understanding.

People say, "But I'm confused. I don't understand."
I say, "That's your concern."
For you must still keep breathing,
even if you're confused,
and you must still eat,
even if you don't understand,
for no one will do these things for you.

Oh, you might get a slave for a while,
but even slaves eventually say,
"When do I get mine?"
And the master always answers, "Later."
And so the slave revolts.

continued

Thirty-seven

continued

But if the slave is smart, it just evolves.
For at that point of evolution,
you find out that the one who has served you
has been your god,
and the one who has understood you
has been your light,
and the one who walks with you
has been the Beloved.
And you never had to go anywhere.

Thirty-eight

I tell you:
you can only be upset and hurt
when you're carrying upset and hurt.

Thirty-nine

The web of our life is of a mingled yarn, good and ill together. Our virtues would be proud if our faults whipped them not, and our crimes would despair if they were not cherished by our virtues.

William Shakespeare

*W*e can be in a state of doing,
or we can be in a state of being.

In a state of being, we don't have to do anything.
All we have to do is just be here.

That's pretty much what the Traveler is.
It's a state of being.
It doesn't have to perform.

We're always doing something,
for good or for bad,
as a necessity of our life.
Then we let these necessities become our focus,
and that becomes our obsession or our compulsion.
Then we spend the rest of the time working through
    obsessions and compulsions.
But there is no way you can work through them
    because they *are* that.

When you come to the state of being, there are no
    compulsions.
Being just expresses itself through you
    as limitless love and energy.
Whatever you do,
you walk in your state of being,
and, therefore,
the action is karmically free.

Forty

*W*atch out when you win an argument.
That means someone else lost.
If you are loving that person,
you are then part of the loss.
If you are not loving that person,
you have your work cut out for you.

As for me,
if there is a conflict with another human being
and someone declares it a win-lose situation,
I'd choose the loss.

I'd rather lose my ego,
my position,
my need to be right
than win.
I'd rather that someone I love learn from their winning
than that I inflict a loss on them.
That's a heavier loss than I'd prefer.

And when it comes right down to it,
there is no such thing as winning or losing.
There is only experience.

If I act out of integrity and loving,
it doesn't matter who is right.
It doesn't even matter what happens.
What does matter is what I have invested inwardly.

continued

<u>Forty</u>
continued

If I am attached to my history of limitations,
which weighs down the present,
I have lost the war even if I win the battle.
If I present myself and my point of view in loving,
with no attachment to the outcome,
I have won before any battle has started.

Forty-one

*H*e wins who endures to the end.
And I've never had that as referring to competition
  with another person.

When I've said it to myself,
I've meant that this one inside me is going to win.
Because when this outer personality gives up
and makes its excuses,
this inner one is still going to continue on,
doing the best it can.

Forty-two

A truly good man does nothing,
Yet leaves nothing undone.
A foolish man is always doing,
Yet much remains to be done.

Lao-Tzu

*I*f we can just be,
   and we can let that being of who we are come
     forward,
   and we can let our voice and our mind just present
     themselves,
   this being will do away with all the doing that has
     been our compulsive and obsessive behavior.

Do you understand this?

That being comes forward,
and then *it* does the doing.
And there's no karma
because the action is done from the state of being,
not from the state of ego,
or from right and wrong
or from "I'm supposed to know"
or anything else like that.

People say, "How do you know these things?"
I reside in the state of being.
They say, "But how do you accomplish so much?"
What I do is done from the state of being,
or I don't do it.

Forty-three

One of the best ways to go faster
is to have more patience
and to progress more gradually.

Things will then be given to you
in a way you can handle.

Forty-four

*I*t matters little what someone else does or has done.
What does matter is what you're doing right now.

It matters very much that you get your head out of
   yesterday
because that is attachment.
So, as many times as you have to "throw water in your
   face"
to bring yourself to today,
you do that.

Do whatever it takes to bring yourself to right now
because you cannot transcend the physical from
   yesterday,
and you can't do it from tomorrow.

Forty-five

Henceforth, please God, forever I forego,
The yoke of men's opinions. I will be
Light-hearted as a bird, and live with God.
I find Him in the bottom of my heart,
I hear continuously His voice therein.

The little needle always knows the North,
The little bird remembereth his note,
And this wise seer within me never errs,
I never taught it what it teaches me;
I only follow, when I act aright.

Ralph Waldo Emerson

*T*here are many things in life you do not have to do.

You do not have to seek love.

You do not have to defend yourself.

You do not have to be noticed.

You do not have to go out and seek the madhouse world of success, fame, and fortune.

You do not have to be what is called a "spiritual person."

You do not have to anxiously hope for anything.

You do not have to be considered nice by others.

You do not have to have to security.

Security lies in the inner awareness
that there is no security.
When you stop fighting for security
and recognize that there is none,
then there is no more concern about that.

Forty-six

*I*f you have the choice
of the divine knowing
or the divine unknowing,
take the divine unknowing.

As soon as you know,
you have to take responsibility for all the actions.
As soon as you don't know,
you still are open to receive of the grace of that.

<u>Forty-seven</u>

*Y*ou take the body, the emotions, the mind, and the
    subconscious,
and you screw up your present reality,
which is perfectly existing right now.

Even your screwing up everything is perfect in its
    existence of being screwed up right now.
That's the paradox of the whole thing,
and that's why nothing is happening.

Your depression, your illness is perfectly manifesting
    right now.
Then you say you need to do something.
Why do anything with it?
Because it's there?
No, it's here.
Being *here*, it's already being taken care of,
but if it's *there*, you can never take care of it,
so forget it.

Right now is the time to partake of everything.
Right now is when the consciousness of reality is
    present.
There is no time when it will be present other than
    right now.
Therefore, you don't have to go anyplace.

Forty-eight

Student, tell me, what is God?
He is the breath inside the breath.

Kabir

*I*f God is going to be called forth,
  you sit and listen.

If you get nothing and it's still,
you must realize that underneath the stillness is the
  Creator,
who is holding the stillness.

So, in everything you do,
  whether failure or success,
you must realize
that God is containing and holding all of that.

Forty-nine

*T*aking on new projects is not necessarily a positive
   change.
It may be a sign of recklessness and nonfulfillment.

But going back to all the levels of noncompletion and
   completing them
is a sign of positive change.

Fifty

*Y*ou can get free of your addictions.
You have been given everything you need to alleviate
    any addiction you have.
You can do it anytime you care to do it
by focusing here and now.

It's a very simple key,
except that your addictions will tell you
that you can't do it that way.
So you must stop listening to that which says it can't
    be done
and start doing it.

This isn't doing everything all at once,
but it *is* doing what comes into your here-and-now
    existence for you to handle here and now.

If you are talking to people while reflecting back to
    last week,
you are splitting yourself.
When you go into this or something similar,
you are going into memory,
and memory isn't what the heart desires.
The heart doesn't want a memory;
it wants a here and now.

Fifty-one

He who knows how to live can walk abroad
Without fear of rhinoceros or tiger.
He will not be wounded in battle.
For in him rhinoceroses can find no place to thrust their horn,
Tigers no place to use their claws,
And weapons no place to pierce.
Why is this so?
Because he has no place for death to enter.

Lao-Tzu

*W*hat does resentment bring to you?
It brings you the feeling of resentment.
And what happens when you think of love?
You get the feeling of love.

Observe your resentment.
As soon as you get above the timeline of it,
nobody can trap you
because you're not going anywhere.
They've got to come to you,
and on their way in,
you can observe them.

When they get there,
you're above time,
so when they go to reach for you,
you're not there
because you are in a state of observation.

Fifty-two

Nothing stands outside your loving.
You love your mistakes along with your successes.
You love the down times as much as the up times.

In other words,
you love yourself through everything,
and your effort goes into loving.

When things happen that may seem unfair at first
   glance,
look for the loving lesson underneath.
If you can't see it there,
put it there yourself
so that you can see everything that happens to you
through the eyes of loving.

Fifty-three

*Y*ou don't have to pretend to be anything.
You can just be ordinary.

You can just breathe your air in
and breath your air out.

You don't have to dramatize.
Just be ordinary.
That is the prior condition to the energy that you
   have conditioned.
That's spiritual.
You can't do it.
It does it.

The reason you can't do it is because
   as soon as you put your mind to it,
you condition the energy,
and then you can't have it.
And as soon as you feel it,
you've conditioned the energy,
and you can't have it.

So you say, "Well, I might just as well let go
   and let God."
That's right.
There's not another way you can get it.

Fifty-four

Being is not what it seems,
nor non-being. The world's
existence is not
in the world.

Rumi

*W*e are so busy playing the game of conditioned
 energy,
that we forget there's a prior condition to all games.

Your conditioning says,
"But I've got to be doing something,
or I'm not spiritual."
But there's nothing there.

When you're sitting in the Divine presence,
it all becomes very humorous
because it's Spirit,
not spiritual.

That presence holds and maintains all universes,
all worlds without end.
All.
The totality.
That's why I've said there's nothing happening,
there's nothing going on.

And so all we really can do
is breathe in and breathe out
and let the Divine essence move forward to us.
It's called grace.

Listen long enough for this breath of Divine guidance
to breathe through you.

Fifty-five

*I*n all of this, the truth resides.

So you don't have to do anything,
and truth still resides,
or you can do everything,
and truth still resides,
because truth is not dependent on
or related to any of your actions.
It is.

And truth we refer to as God,
Divine presence.
It's just here.

Then why a Mystical Traveler?
Because you didn't know about that
    until you were told.

Fifty-six

*S*ometimes you forget to declare things done,
   so there are little incomplete energies
   that just keep floating around and draining off a little
      energy
   every time they come up.

You may be going down the road,
   doing fine, feeling good,
   and all of a sudden
   some incident from the past comes up
   and grabs your attention.

You say, "Wow! Where did that come from?
   I haven't thought of that in years.
   How did that get in there?"

Your inner beingness brings these up
   for you to deal with and clear.

Fifty-seven

What I most want
is to spring out of this personality,
then to sit apart from that leaping.
I've lived too long where I can be reached.

Rumi

*I*f you don't know what's going on,
how can you possibly doubt it?
All you are is impatient to get it.
And your impatience is distracting you
from your here-and-now life.

You don't do anything with impatience.
Impatience is doing it.
You just observe it.

When you observe, you reach a state of contentment.
That state of contentment allows the Soul energy to
activate through you.
When you start riding back on that energy to the
center inside of you,
you get past time.

Fifty-eight

isten carefully:

All your problems have been because
you moved from your own center
into something that the mind conjured up.
But this consciousness can never be pleased.

You think you've got to go someplace.
But there is no place to go,
and there is nothing when you get there.

Nothing that you did in the last thirty seconds
   or before
has any control over you at all,
and none of it matters.

There are a lot of people around you who are going to
   try to run the past on you
because they run it on themselves.
And you can just say, "That's past!"

Fifty-nine

I came into this world, not chiefly to make this a good place to live in, but to live in it, be it good or bad.

Henry David Thoreau

*N*eutrality is a progressive, assertive statement of
    your being,
without attachment to results
or to the process of getting someplace.

It's enough that you are here,
enjoying things.

No matter what someone else does,
you continue to express from your loving heart.
That is neutrality.

<u>Sixty</u>

*C*an't you just spend a little time with me?
Can't you just forsake this world for a little time,
and come in to where you are?

You get in there for a little bit,
and things straighten out quite well.
Then you're off,
gallivanting around,
and you forsake the very thing that you are.

Yet you must get it so full inside of you
that no matter where you go and what you do,
that is always there.

Those who realize God consciousness are those who
enter into it,
hold to it,
and maintain it
as the one thing they must never forget.

Sixty-one

JAQUES: *Rosalind is your love's name?*
ORLANDO: *Yes, just.*
JAQUES: *I do not like her name.*
ORLANDO: *There was no thought of pleasing you when she was christened.*

William Shakespeare

*D*o not attempt to keep up with anyone.
Don't even attempt to keep up with yourself
    because your Self is going nowhere.
It's present.
Here it is.

There is no right to be earned here.
It is given to us by grace.
Therein lies the difference.
The only true right we have is our own inheritance,
and we don't have to go anywhere
because we've already inherited.

That inheritance is absolute truth.
It resides upon itself in itself,
not dependent upon anybody's point of view
or whether they like it or not.

Sixty-two

How, then, do we live in this world?
How can we gain?
What can our goal be?

For God's sake,
don't have a goal in this world.
It's going to beat you bloody.

Where is the goal?
The goal is inside.
When you turn back inside,
you have your goal,
you have your completeness,
you have your fullness
and you walk through the world,
having all else added unto you.

<u>Sixty-three</u>

*F*ind the harmony.

Life is as simple as breathing in and breathing out.
Once you find the rhythm of that,
you can follow it through.

If you could gain just that discipline
and hold it,
you would start overcoming all this physical world.

Sixty-four

The pleasures of heaven are with me, and the pains of
  hell are with me,
The first I graft and increase upon myself...the latter I
  translate into a new tongue.

Walt Whitman

*A*t the moment that we're contracting
(perhaps somebody hurt our feelings),
and we are tightening in and down,
at that moment we have to cut the knot of
    contraction
and expand.

Any attachment—love or hate—
is going to cause suffering.

If you love or hate "out there,"
you do it inside you.
That's where the suffering is.

So, inside me, I just love a lot.
If people project negativity,
by the time it gets through my field of energy,
it's loving.
So I get to *hear* what they are saying
without *feeling* what they are saying.

It takes a lot of practice.
You've got to walk up to that field of negative contact
and stand with it
and hold and hold
until you can start becoming loving and positive in it.

continued

Sixty-four

continued

What you do is sacrifice all your positions.
Sacrifice your thoughts, your emotions, and your
  body.
Just become loving,
and let them say what they want to.

Sixty-five

*I*f you complete everything that's coming your way
    now,
then, when you look back,
you won't have memory.
You will see only the results of progression.

We have memory when we have uncompleted things.
But there is nothing in existence other than right
    now.
When we go into memory,
we're no longer present in the Spirit.
We're in a contraction of the mind and emotions,
and it has no value for us.

Sixty-six

*D*o you understand the idea of staying present?

In the immediate present,
right now,
there is nothing in existence that you cannot handle.

However, you can create hallucinatory figments "out
    there"
that you cannot handle.
Nobody can handle them from here
because they are not real.
But if they drop into realness in the physical world and
    come into you,
you can handle them at that time.

It doesn't matter how you get through things.
It matters only that you get through them.

Sixty-seven

Yet soul be sure the first intent remains, and shall be carried out,
Perhaps even now the time has arrived.

Walt Whitman

*N*ot one Soul is going to be lost.
In fact, there aren't any lost Souls.
The Soul always knows where it is.
It just doesn't care.

The Soul knows it is going to outlast your body,
it knows it's going to outlast the thoughts you've been
   having,
it knows it's going to go beyond the imagination,
and your feelings have betrayed you for so long that
   it pays little attention to them.
So why shouldn't it be happy in these lower worlds?

Our misidentification causes us to go into the
   quandary of the mind to second-guess.
And yet the Soul says,
"I'm here, I'm present.
I'm not over there.
I'm here, I'm present.
This is the moment."

<u>Sixty-eight</u>

*W*e say, "Hitch your wagon to a star,"
but make that star high in the heavens.

When you get that high,
you can see all the others,
and you can see correctly where things are.

You can see what the world is.
You can see the delusions of mankind
and the inhumanities that we perpetrate against
  the physical form,
attempting to control it.

But behind the prison bars of the body, the emotions,
  and the mind
stands the freedom of the consciousness that is pure.

So, you can make me say all sorts of things,
you can beat me,
you can lock me up and crucify me,
but beyond even all that,
I will be free in where I live,
and there's no way you can touch that.

I can tell you anything I want to tell you,
but in my Soul I am free,
and that's where I'm going to reside.

Sixty-nine

*Y*ou can become free in this Soul that cannot be
   grasped,
that cannot be contained,
for it is the very breath with which you breathe.

You can't continue to expel your breath,
nor can you hold it and make it stay,
for it does what it wants to do,
according to its own timing.

If you get in the timing of that which is always
   present,
and you flow with it in the naturalness of love,
the physical disturbances fall away,
and you are free.

Seventy

Because the sage always confronts difficulties,
He never experiences them.

Lao-Tzu

*W*e can solve our problems rapidly
by making the supportive decision at the moment,
not after the occurrence.

Deciding after the occurrence
is the approach of the intellect.

The intelligence, however, tells you to keep aware,
keep awake,
keep flowing with the present,
and keep making the decisions that enhance your
    positive expression and your spiritual fulfillment.

Love is the key—
total, unconditional love.
Even when you don't feel like loving,
you love the feeling of not feeling like loving.

Love yourself
even when you don't know what is going on.
You can be everything you want to be
as soon as you unconditionally become unconditional.

There is no way you can separate yourself from love
    and maintain freedom.
The only way is to love it all.

Seventy-one

*H*ow do you accomplish things without getting
 karma?

By spontaneously having the action and the energy
 come forward through you to accomplish
 for the highest good of all—
without ego involvement in the goal, the results, or
 the outcome.

When the energy of Spirit moves through you to
 accomplish,
It is the doer of whatever takes place,
not you.

What is accomplished through Spirit
and what is accomplished through ego
may appear to be the same,
but the one who moved with the ego has karma,
and the one who moved spontaneously with the
 action of Spirit
is karma-free.

Seventy-two

There's majesty and there's beauty in everyone.
If you could see it in yourself,
you would not hassle yourself over that little bit of
    food,
over that little bit of drink,
over that little bit of cigarette,
over this or over that,
or where the next sex is coming from,
or your occupation for the next fifty years.

Instead, you would be totally in this moment,
in the divine Presence—
not as an empty vessel,
but as one where your cup runs over
and you don't have to tilt it to give to anyone,
but it just flows over
because you're in the very beingness of reality.

All that the spiritual force has asked of the human
    form is to love unconditionally,
to love each other as you'd love yourself,
to love God with all your heart, your mind, your Soul,
and, if you don't know where God is,
to love your neighbor.

But some of you love God whom you can't see,
and hate your neighbor whom you can see,
and that's hypocrisy.

Seventy-three

In the pursuit of learning, every day something is acquired.
In the pursuit of Tao, every day something is dropped.

Less and less is done
Until non-action is achieved.
When nothing is done, nothing is left undone.

The world is ruled by letting things take their course.
It cannot be ruled by interfering.

Lao-Tzu

When you place a goal out there in the world,
you must perform according to the legend of success.
And who is going to determine that for you?
Everybody out there in the world will determine it.

Yet your very success may be that you give up the goal
and don't do it.
Some people will "hit you in the head" for that thought.
But, often, my best successes have been when I said,
"I can't handle that,"
and I let it go.

Then I was brought immediately
to the very thing that I was to do,
and it was better than I ever could have wished for.

Seventy-four

*M*any who have told the truth on this planet have
    been assassinated and martyred.
And yet they stood forward and said,
"For such as it is, this is it."

We have to come to that one ourselves.
We have to look in the mirror and say,
"This is it.
There may be more here,
but since I don't know that,
this is what I'm going to work with right now.
This is what has been created.
Here I am.
I'm not going to declare a world of events
or how I'm going to do in the next twenty years.
Just right now."

Seventy-five

To make a big effort is a fighting situation.

As soon as you set up fighting,
you set up resistance.
As soon as you make an effort,
you set up defense.

Defense blocks.

To just naturally reach and take the next thing
and pull it to you
and move with it
in a very even-flowing way
is an accepting situation.

Seventy-six

But who, if he be called upon to face
Some awful moment to which Heaven has
    joined
Great issues, good or bad for humankind,
Is happy as a lover.

William Wordsworth

*A*nyone can play the game.

As a matter of fact,
almost everyone plays the game
except the man of understanding.

He goes through the routine with you
and laughs
and has a good time,
and you can't understand why he's not serious about
    this.

It's because he understands that there is nothing to be
    serious about,
because the whole divine action of God
is entirely present.

And so this man of understanding is accused of being
    everything
but understanding.

Seventy-seven

*A*waken to the very Light that you already are.

Instead of trying to set up your kingdom in God's
   kingdom and trying to overthrow God,
become aware that God is already present.

That awareness is a process of letting God do it.
Then when you say, "Let go and let God,"
you'll find out that God has been doing it all anyway,
even when you weren't letting go.

Seventy-eight

*S*ometimes the one who is your friend appears
   to be your enemy.
And often your enemies can appear to be your
   friends.
You know the difference by observing them,
and you observe them with detachment.

Relationships are difficult
because most of the time
we find the person's weakness and play on it.

Seventy-nine

The wind blows wherever it pleases.
You hear its sound
but you cannot tell where it comes from
or where it is going.
So it is with everyone born of the Spirit.

Jesus Christ
John 3:8 (NIV)

*U*nderstanding is the moving of the reality that is
   present,
the divineness of its own self,
the truth that resides upon nothing,
that which can be the whirlwind,
that which blows the wind,
and that which quiets it.

And so you don't know if you're coming,
or if you're going,
or if you're caught in the whirlwind.

But if you are in the consciousness of understanding,
what difference does it make?
It is all the divineness.

<u>Eighty</u>

*S*ome people become disturbed about their
    compulsions.
But it's really their *thoughts* about the
    compulsion that bother them.
So if you stop thinking about the compulsion
    and call it, "That's what it is,"
and go about your business,
you no longer give energy to that which will corrupt
    you.
And so it falls way.

<u>Eighty-one</u>

*E*ven though the things we do in this physical world
may continually misrepresent who we are,
let's never forget for even one second
that the divine spark that is God
resides within each one of us.

And after all has been said and done,
you'll find out that you've been walking with
  your own Beloved
for many, many eons.
And one of your great realizations will be that,
at all times,
everything was absolutely perfect within you.

If you have a spirit, lose it,
loose it to return where with one word,
we came from. Now, thousands of words,
and we refuse to leave.

Rumi

ACKNOWLEDGMENTS

Our thanks to the following who allowed their translations to appear in this book:

Kabir quotes were from:
The Kabir Book by Robert Bly
Copyright © 1971, 1977 by Robert Bly
Reprinted by permission of Beacon Press

Rumi quotes were from :
Unseen Rain
Quatrains of Rumi by John Moyne and Coleman Barks
Reprinted by permission of
Threshold Books
RD4 Box 600
Putney, VT 05346

Lao-Tzu quotes were from:
Tao Te Ching by Gia-fu Feng/Jane English
Copyright © 1972 by Gia-fu Feng and Jane English
Reprinted by permission of Alfred E. Knopf, Inc

ABOUT THE AUTHOR

Since 1963, John-Roger has traveled all over the world, lecturing, teaching, and assisting people who want to create a life of greater health, happiness, peace, and prosperity and a greater awakening to the Spirit within. His humor and practical wisdom have benefited thousands and lightened many a heart.

In the course of this work, he has given over 4,000 seminars, many of which are televised nationally on "That Which Is.: He has also written more than 20 books, including co-authoring the *New York Times* #1 best-seller *DO IT!* and the best-selling *You Can't Afford the Luxury of a Negative Thought.*

The common thread throughout all John-Roger's work is loving, opening to the highest good of all, and the awareness that God is abundantly present and available.

If you've enjoyed this book, you may want to explore and delve more deeply into what John-Roger has shared about this subject and other related topics. Here is a short selection of study materials. For a wider selection of study materials and more information on John-Roger's teachings through MSIA, please contact us at:

MSIA
P.O. Box 3935
Los Angeles, CA 90051
(213) 737-4055.

Walking with the Lord

$12.50—Paperbound Book

This book is for anyone who is interested in finding out more about one of the most essential parts of the teachings of the Mystical Traveler—spiritual exercises. It contains specific information and techniques as well as encouragement and guidance.

Forgiveness

The Key to the Kingdom

12.50—Paperbound Book

A treasure house of inspiration, reading this book centers us in our hearts and assists us to regenerate our strength and purpose in life.

Health from the Inside Out

$24.95—Three audiotape packet

A beautifully presented tape packet in which John-Roger dynamically explores health as an aspect of our consciousness. The icing on the cake is a relaxing Body Balance Meditation by John-Roger which is designed to be played over and over again.

Soul Awareness Discourses

$100—A course of study (one year)

Soul Awareness Discourses are the heart of the teachings offered through MSIA. A yearly set consists of twelve books, one for each month. They offer keys to greater spiritual awareness and knowledge of the Soul, as well as many practical keys to more successful living.